FREDDY KRUEGER

Fly!

abdobooks.com

Published by Abdo Zoom, a division of ABDO, P.O. Box 398166, Minneapolis, Minnesota 55439. Copyright © 2020 by Abdo Consulting Group, Inc. International copyrights reserved in all countries. No part of this book may be reproduced in any form without written permission from the publisher. Fly!™ is a trademark and logo of Abdo Zoom.

Printed in the United States of America, North Mankato, Minnesota.
052019
092019

THIS BOOK CONTAINS
RECYCLED MATERIALS

Photo Credits: Alamy, Everette Collection
Production Contributors: Kenny Abdo, Jennie Forsberg, Grace Hansen
Design Contributors: Dorothy Toth, Neil Klinepier

Library of Congress Control Number: 2018963570

Publisher's Cataloging-in-Publication Data

Names: Abdo, Kenny, author.
Title: Freddy Krueger / by Kenny Abdo.
Description: Minneapolis, Minnesota : Abdo Zoom, 2020 | Series: Hollywood monsters set 2 | Includes online resources and index.
Identifiers: ISBN 9781532127458 (lib. bdg.) | ISBN 9781532128431 (ebook) | ISBN 9781532128929 (Read-to-me ebook)
Subjects: LCSH: Krueger, Freddy (Fictitious character)--Juvenile literature. | Nightmare on Elm Street (Motion picture : 1984)--Juvenile literature. | Horror films--Juvenile literature. | Motion picture characters--Juvenile literature.
Classification: DDC 791.43616--dc23

TABLE OF CONTENTS

FREDDY KRUEGER

A Nightmare on Elm Street is a movie about a killer named Freddy Krueger. He dies at the hands of a town's angry parents. As revenge, he goes after their children. He murders them in their dreams!

5

From his iconic glove of knives to his even sharper wit, Freddy Krueger has given the kids of Elm Street and the world a serious case of **insomnia**!

ORIGIN

Filmmaker Wes Craven based the movie's plot on a news report. A random group of young men died in their sleep while having nightmares. They had no previous history of health problems.

Craven also used a memory from when he was 10 years old. Looking out his window, he saw a man dressed in a red sweater and hat staring up at him. The man was so scary, that he was Craven's **muse** for Freddy.

Craven named his movie monster
Freddy Krueger. That was the name
of a boy who bullied him in school.

HOLLYWOOD

Wes Craven **pitched** *A Nightmare on Elm Street* to many studios. It was rejected by all of them. The independent studio, New Line Cinema, gave it a chance.

Classically trained actor Robert Englund
played Krueger. Heather Langenkamp
beat over two hundred actresses for the
role of Nancy Thompson.

It took Englund three hours to get into make up. Krueger is in the movie for only about seven minutes.

"I knew it was a good film when it was scary on **set** when they were filming," Producer Rachel Talalay said. "...[Y]ou're looking at pieces of rubber and it's still scary."

A Nightmare on Elm Street was a smash hit! New Line Cinema was saved from **bankruptcy** by its success. Later, the studio was nicknamed "The House that Freddy Built."

LEGACY

Freddy became a pop culture icon! His face can be found on albums, t-shirts, and many novels. A TV show, *Freddy's Nightmares*, ran for 44 episodes. There was even a hotline you could call to hear Freddy threaten you!

Freddy starred in eight more movies.
Freddy Vs. Jason pitted the two slashers
against each other in 2003.

A *Nightmare on Elm Street* is considered one of the most successful horror series of all time. The franchise has grossed more than $450 million dollars.

GLOSSARY

bankrupt – legally lacking funds needed to pay off money owed.

franchise – a collection of related movies in a series.

gross – to make a profit.

hotline – a telephone line set up for a certain purpose.

icon – a person or thing regarded as a representative of something.

insomnia – the inability to sleep.

muse – a person who is the inspiration for an artist.

pitch – an idea for a movie by a screenwriter or producer.

role – a part an actor plays.

set – an artificial setting where a movie or television program is filmed.

ONLINE RESOURCES

Booklinks
NONFICTION NETWORK
FREE! ONLINE NONFICTION RESOURCES

To learn more about
Freddy Krueger, please visit
abdobooklinks.com or scan
this QR code. These links
are routinely monitored and
updated to provide the most
current information available.

INDEX